AF429714

Embracing God's Amazing Grace
The Place Where Love And Abundance Reside

Kevin Hartdige

And [I pray] that the eyes of your heart [the very center and core of your being] may be enlightened [flooded with light by the Holy Spirit], so that you will know and cherish the hope [the divine guarantee, the confident expectation] to which He has called you, the riches of His glorious inheritance in the saints (God's people), and [so that you will begin to know] what the immeasurable and unlimited and surpassing greatness of His [active, spiritual] power is in us who believe.

—Ephesians 1:18–19 AMP

TABLE OF CONTENTS

FOREWORD

I first met Kevin in the fall of 1996. My family and I had just moved to the Denver suburb of Aurora, Colorado, and started attending a church where Kevin led the worship. Kevin and I also share a rare distinction as friends. During the early days of our friendship, Kevin became the pastor of the church we were attending and so became my pastor. Several years later I planted a church in the southeast metro area of Denver, which Kevin and his family chose to call home. And I became his pastor.

From the first moment I met Kevin, I could tell that there was something uniquely and refreshingly human about him. It was more than his talent as a musician, although he is wildly talented. What drew me to Kevin, and still does, is his sincerity as a person, a friend, and in this case, an author. Sincerity and perfection are often at odds in our lives, seemingly engaged in an exhausting game of tug-of-war. But, to know Kevin is to realize that this exhausting paradox can be resolved by accepting the reality of this apparent conundrum. The fact is there is no true sincerity in perfection; there is just performance. True sincerity can only emerge from the crucible of imperfection, from the lessons learned in trying to perform our way through life. Sincerity is available to us when we exchange doing for being.

Sincerity: the quality of being free from pretense, deceit, or hypocrisy.

I believe Kevin's ability to look at life through a lens tempered by genuineness and candor, forged by the fires of imperfection, is what makes him such an engaging and insightful writer. This book, *Embracing God's Amazing Grace*, cuts through the pretenses and performances that have served to water down much of the Christian experience in the twenty-first century. Written from a place of personal experience, Kevin invites the reader to walk with him along a path of authentic discovery of what it has always meant to live in God, empowered by His amazing grace. Even his choice of tense inspires the reader to embrace the reality that this is a new day, a new time, and a new opportunity, as if drawing on the power of Apostle Paul in Philippians, "forgetting what lies behind I press on." From the opening introduction where he invites readers to reflect on who they truly are, to painting a vivid and empowering picture of the true nature of Christ, and ending with an inspiring reminder of how we see and are seen by God, *Embracing God* refreshes us every step of the way.

It may be out of the ordinary to thank the author for the invitation to write the foreword of his book, but as I stated earlier, this is no ordinary friendship. So, thank you, Kevin Hartdige, for this unique opportunity. Your lifelong devotion to the discovery of what it means to be in God comes across with an undeniable and piercing clarity in this book. Any reader who is serious about shedding the shackles of a performance-based relationship with a God of the past and created in man's image will find renewed inspiration in this book. To you, my friend and brother, continue your hot pursuit of what is genuine and alive, never settling for mere reflections and that which is only reminiscent of the past. Life in God is vibrant, new, and expanding. It always has been and it always will be!

—Ed Barron

INTRODUCTION

When looking into a mirror, you are immediately confronted with the physical features that are used to identify you. Those features are also what allow others to recognize and identify who you are. Looking into a mirror, some may not be happy with the reflection staring back at them. In some cases they may be able to cosmetically alter their appearance to reveal what they believe is a more pleasing person. Who we are, however, is comprised of more than just the physical features people can see. The totality of our being consists of our morals, our beliefs, our unique characteristics, and our attitudes. They involve our mind, our soul, and our spirit, and ultimately, they are reflected in our conversation and our behavior.

What cannot be immediately seen or reflected in the mirror is the identity of your soul and spirit. When you begin to speak and act, others can see who you are or, at least, who it is you want them to see. The same questions still apply: Do you like what you see, who you are, in your identity that is being reflected and emanating from your soul and spirit? Is the truth about who you are (your identity) being shown to the world? Do you even understand and know who you are as an individual, or are you unknowingly searching to know yourself? If you are unhappy with who you are, I suggest that there is an emptiness, a void that you are looking to be filled. You may try different things—jobs, churches, mates, drugs, or friends—in order to feel satisfied, fulfilled, and happy with who you are.

It would seem that the whole of our lives is spent trying to discover who we are. I see this as a search for identity, much of which may be unconscious. Mainly because, even though many of us know there is a noticeable and seemingly unquenchable void in our lives, we have struggled to pinpoint what it is that is missing. We spend much of our lives looking to and emulating others, choosing to identify ourselves with the charisma, the notoriety, or the mystique that others possess. We look to groups, to movements, to organizations, to our families, and to friends to tell us who we are. The behaviors that we exemplify during much of our lives may truly be masking our true identity, signifying that there is a serious disconnect in our ability to determine and embrace who we are. Unfortunately, behaviors—good, bad, or indifferent—will elicit others to identify us with their labels, and, as a result, we perform accordingly.

Most human beings are desirous of attaching meaning and purpose to their lives. At some level, many believe they are here in the universe to accomplish something by making a difference in the world and in the lives of others. At an early age children are asked what they want to do for a living, or what they want to be when they grow up. This is typically in reference to obtaining a job or career that will give them financial stability, fulfillment, and happiness. This type of conversation with children should be had in conjunction with a good understanding of their personality, their interests, and their abilities. There are a number of assessments, such as DISC and Briggs-Myers that are used to help individuals uncover their most dominant personality traits and align them with specific career paths. If they are used, it could enhance the chance that some will discover their personality, their passion, and their purpose. The collision of personality, passion, and purpose at just the right time forms three necessary components that assist us in realizing who we are, thereby propelling us to our destiny.

CHAPTER 1 IN THE BEGINNING

My birth certificate identifies me as Kevin L. Hartdige, a Negro male born to Melvin and Lois Hartdige at UCLA Medical Center in Los Angeles, California. All human beings are uniquely created, fashioned in the womb of a woman. Our bodies are proof of our physical existence. We are identified and distinguished by our name, our ethnicity, our gender, and distinguishable features, such as eye color, hair color, ears, nose and lips, our DNA, and our fingerprints. These are the identifiers that tell people who we are at a glance via the senses. This is the surface level or physical part of our identity. But the essence of who we are goes deeper than what we can see, touch, and smell on the outside.

Humans are triune beings: body, soul, and spirit. There is something deep within our soul and spirit that seeks acceptance, value, and worth. The value and worth we assign to ourselves or that others assign to us are part of our makeup and fuel our existence in a positive or negative way. Value and worth are usually assigned early in childhood by our parents. When parents fail to let their children know they have value and worth, they are left to figure out their value and worth on their own. In many instances you may find that those children will have deficiencies and, in some cases, an inability to feel accepted.

During our formative years, our morals and beliefs are also being forged in our hearts and minds by our parents. This usually occurs through parental mandates—through the teachings and discipline, or lack of discipline, from those parents. As we continue to grow and mature, we connect with others who become role models and influencers in our lives. Our morals and beliefs are confirmed and cemented through some, and further developed and enhanced through others. These people may be pastors, teachers, policemen, aunts, uncles, or friends. They will either build upon the foundation established by our parents, or they will serve to tear down that foundation. The result will be a delay in our arrival at our true identity destination, or, an enhancement of our chances of finding and embracing our true identity. At this stage of our development, we see life through the eyes of all of these individuals. There is an abundance of information that we receive via learning, the opinions of others, and the ideologies and beliefs that have been downloaded into our memory banks. As we continue to grow and mature, we begin to form our own opinions, discarding some beliefs and determining what is moral or immoral for ourselves.

In my own personal beginning and journey, much of what was formulated in my mind that encompassed who I was and how I behaved was formulated early on by my mom and the teachings of the Protestant Church. I grew up believing that God is the source of all life according to Colossians 1:15–20. That man, who was created in the image of God (Genesis 1:27), rebelled against Him in the garden. Man's rebellion infected all mankind with sin and created a breach between us and God. As a result, Jesus Christ gave His life to pay the required penalty of Adam's sin and redeem humankind. These beliefs are the foundation upon which I have lived my life. My worth, my value, and all I was living for was wrapped up in the Church and all that it taught. My identity was tied to my performance in the Church and my behavior outside of the Church. Everything I did, I did to gain acceptance with people and to gain favor with God. I was identified as a Christian, a follower of Christ, and a disciple of Christ, and to the best of my ability (heart, mind, and strength) I acted accordingly, living my life by trying to meet the expectations of others. My gifts caused those who knew me to prophesy and identify me as a preacher and an eventual pastor. Even with all of this, something was still missing in my life. It was becoming increasingly and painfully apparent that all I was doing as a Christian was not only not enough, but also would never be enough to erase my uncertainty about who I was. My true identity was lost on me.

CHAPTER 2 **NEVER ENOUGH**

One can understand and agree that good moral character and behavior are a good start to one living a long and fulfilled life. One can come to believe in the finished work of Jesus Christ (His death, burial, and resurrection) as the redeemer and reconciler of humankind to God the Father, and that this belief is the key to knowing where one will spend eternity. One can earn college degrees; have a successful career; get married and raise a family; buy a big house in the city, country, or suburbs—all of the things that are supposed to define success and bring us happiness—and still be empty. Many of these things may give us an initial euphoria, an initial high that may provide temporary satisfaction. For some of us, however, they end up being nothing more than burdens to bear as we try to keep up with the Joneses. All of these things do not define who we are; they are just the things we do as part of our existence in this life. They are based on what we think we want, and what we think we know and understand about ourselves, those around us, and our Creator. Many of us may be hard pressed to find anyone in or out of our immediate sphere of influence who could say with any certainty that with all they have gained and accomplished, they are fulfilled, happy, and at peace. Without a good understanding of our true identity in terms of our inner being, we will consistently struggle to operate our lives at their intended capacity and purpose. When we meet people and introduce ourselves, the conversation immediately shifts to the question, "What do you do for a living?" I'm a mail carrier; I'm a customer service representative; I'm a financial management analyst; I'm a pastor. These are titles that identify how we earn an income but are not necessarily representative of who we are as individuals. One can have all of these external things, and yet the essence of who we are — our inner being — will still be longing to know its true purpose for existing: communion with God.

Even though I had accepted Christ as my Lord and Savior, neither my relationship with Him nor going to church were enough. As far back as I can remember, I have attended church. It has always been a huge part of my life. Attending Sunday worship services, Sunday school, Wednesday night Bible study, and Friday night services; singing in the choir; heading and participating in various auxiliaries; giving tithes and offerings; and even leading a ministry as a pastor—these are the things the Christian Church has in mind when they talk about people giving of their time, talent, and treasure. I have come to understand that at their best these things amount to religion, which speaks to human effort. Not that these things are bad, in and of themselves, but I could present to you a flock of people (pun intended) who have done all of the above listed items and still long for something more. At the end of the day, the human effort I exerted in checking off all of the Christian Church boxes and trying to live free from sin left me without joy and without peace. It left me tired, worn-out, and confused. Tired and worn-out because it is a system of rules, regulations, dos and don'ts that kept me on the hamster wheel in a cycle of doing, sinning, confessing, and repenting. Repeat. I was confused because it did not make sense that I would be given a gift that could be lost and that I had to work so hard to maintain. Unbeknownst to the Christian Church, it has created a system that promotes our striving for our own righteousness, our own justification, and our own salvation just to stay in the game. Then when you fail to attain and maintain, you're told, "No one's perfect." That's some consolation. So, you console yourself and keep on trying, striving to be good enough. Despite our best efforts, it seems we can never measure up to anyone's expectations. So what are we doing? What's the point?

CHAPTER 3 WHAT'S THE POINT?

It was around 1998 when I found myself asking this seemingly simple question. I could not connect the dots of the first century with the dots of what was then the twentieth century. It was an impossible gap to bridge in terms of trying to grasp the meaning of my identity with relation to Christ and the Church. This disconnect was palpable. Those who laid claim to being the "light of the world" and the "salt of the earth" seemed to be more representative of the Pharisees than of Christ. Why are there so many churches and so many denominations? Why can't we all just get along? How does the world see us? As I saw and understood things, Christ was the common denominator to our salvation. It seemed like we would allow Him to be the catalyst for breaking down the denominational barriers and traditions that has confronted us and thwarted our desire or willingness in coming to the unity of the faith, according to Ephesians 4. I wanted to know if this was all there was to Christianity. If Christ had come that we might have life more abundantly, was my life a reflection of what He intended in that statement? (John 10:10)

Congregations across the United States are conditioned to believe that although they are saved by grace through faith (Ephesians 2:8), they are ultimately responsible for the remainder of their lives for maintaining their salvation. This immediately causes you to start your Christian journey at a disadvantage. On the one hand, you try to depend on the Holy Spirit for your sanctification, but on the other hand you do everything humanly possible to stay saved and not lose your salvation. This is done by attending church on Sunday and then throughout the week by staying away from people who don't know Christ, so as to not be unequally yoked—by staying away from places and things in the world deemed off-limits by the Church. If you are found to have committed a "don't," your progress is derailed, your sin separates you from God, and you get to start all over again from scratch: confess, repent, rinse. When you are part of a religion that is devoid of understanding the grace of God and all its beauty, you seek your own righteousness, which will never be enough. For me it was never enough because my value and worth were tied to my performance, always falling short of an elusive standard, called "holiness" that was just out of reach. Religion was very successful in rehearsing my shortcomings and my failures, which always kept me at a place of insecurity and fear. It made sure I continued to throw myself on the altar of sacrifice, seeking God's mercy and forgiveness. No abundant life to be found, anywhere.

Unfortunately, what I had come to believe God required from me as a condition of my salvation was really no more than a flawed interpretation of God's word and an incomplete understanding of the truth and significance of the sacrifice of our Lord. One of the things that keeps religion strong is a fear of failing to measure up, a fear that keeps us religiously seeking our own righteousness. Religion causes us to focus on the efforts (behaviors) of others to see how we measure up in our endeavors to be holy. You can always point to someone whom you perceive to be more spiritual than you—one who gives more, who attends more services; he or she is the gold standard. Then there are those people whom you are convinced are not doing as well as you are in their sanctification journey. Remember the saying "I am not what I want to be but, thank God, I am not what I used to be"? Well, when you are trying to be the first one across the finish line to perfection, you look at the people around you and they become the gauge of your standing in Christ. So not only does our value and worth become hinged to how well we perform, but it also becomes tied to successes and failures of our fellow Christians. When we do not know who we are, we see our identity through the eyes of doing, instead of how our Lord sees us. It ignores the fact that our value and worth are tied to Christ and all that He accomplished for us at Calvary.

The point is that we can all be vulnerable to the influence of others who—sometimes consciously, sometimes unconsciously—put their own spin on who they think we are, or even who they might want us to be, molding us in their image. We see a sampling of this in the movie *The Lion King*. Scar, the villain who covets his brother Mufasa's throne, convinces his nephew Simba that his actions alone are to be blamed for his father's death. Simba does not realize that not only was his uncle responsible for his father's death, but also that the death of his father automatically made him the heir to the throne. Scar's deceit convinces Simba that to go back to the pride would mean he would be identified as a murderer. Simba, as the son of Mufasa, had already been identified as king. Not knowing who he was, along with his uncle's prodding, caused Simba to essentially abdicate the throne, thereby bringing unintended consequences to the entire jungle and the pride over which his father had presided. Adam, who doubted who he already was in relation to God, started this abdication way back in the garden. He chose fear over love, choosing to be identified with Lucifer and self-preservation instead of being identified with the One in whose image he had been created. We all know that the effects of his decision became the gift that kept on giving.

The point is that until one comes to believe in the finished work of Christ, the world is the dictator of how life is lived. The standard by which the world lives is dictated by selfishness. Christ is love, and those who are in Christ should be selfless in love. The reality is that even as Christians we struggle to identify with the One who saved us and all that encompasses. As a result, we tend to function in similar fashion to the world. We spend much of our lives seeking

to find something or someone that will bring us a modicum of satisfaction and happiness. We tend to believe that all of our hard work in living a saved life should merit happiness. Until I began to understand the grace of God and the magnitude of His amazing love, I was hopelessly bound by fear and not sure that God had my best interest at heart. I sought to make others happy through my performance and expected to be loved in return. I loved to be seen by others as anointed and gifted. Even though I downplayed it then, I can see now that I very much enjoyed the praises I received. Even as a preteen, people told me I was going to be a preacher. Embracing that identification of what others were saying about me, I surely became driven to fulfill that expectation, whether or not God was saying the same about me. I sought peace, love, and joy through jobs, relationships, and church. At some point, I became exhausted because the masks I wore could no longer hide my dissatisfaction. I was simply a hypocrite, waiting in the wings of a theater, trying to decide which mask to choose before going on stage to coincide with my next performance. Talk about being lost in the sauce. That was me. The point is I did not know who I was. I, like others, was known by what I did, not realizing that how I behaved did not determine who I was, but that knowing my identity would determine how I lived my life.

CHAPTER 4 WHO DO YOU SAY I AM?

The past has a way of holding us in bondage not only to what others think about us, but also to how we think about ourselves. It has the uncanny ability to remind us of all of our past mistakes and failures and keep us trapped in a belief system that keeps us blind about who we really are, thereby denying us the freedom and joy that comes with embracing our identity in Christ. When Christ comes into our lives, He frees us from our past, relieving us of our old self and giving us a new identity. "Therefore if anyone is in Christ, he is a new creature; the old things passed away, behold, new things have come" (2 Corinthians 5:17 NASB). For some, embracing our new identity happens instantly. For others, it can be a slow process of being totally freed from the power that sin can hold over our lives. It enslaves us through fear and the belief that eventually we will run out of chances from God—causing us to constantly look over our shoulders, waiting for the other shoe to drop and being found out that we are not who others think we are and that God has chosen to turn his back on us. Fortunately and mercifully, our sins are not counted against us, and He'll never leave nor forsake us. "Namely, that God was in Christ reconciling the world to Himself, not counting their trespasses against them, and He has committed to us the word of reconciliation" (2 Corinthians 5:19 NASB).

I believe we see a good example of Christ's love in His response to the woman brought to Him because she was caught in the very act of adultery. Jesus's act of mercy and grace toward her changed her life. "Straightening up, Jesus said to her, 'Woman, where are they? Did no one condemn you?' She said, 'No one, Lord.' And Jesus said, 'I do not condemn you, either. Go. From now on sin no more'" (John 8:10–11 NASB). He is essentially removing the stigma associated with her adulterous behavior, essentially changing her identity and saying she is no longer defined by past behaviors. She was now free to live in His mercy and His amazing grace. One of the tendencies we as humans have is our ability to remember and identify others by an act of impropriety that never seems to go away; it is a dark cloud that lingers for the remainder of their lives. When Christ comes into our lives, we no longer have to live in and under that condemnation. If we embrace what Christ did for us the way this woman embraced what He did for her on that fateful day, we will walk into a freedom that is inexplicable to others, but to us, it is everything that grace is meant to be. According to the law, she had a death sentence, but Christ commuted it right there on the spot. We, too, had a death sentence because of sin, and Christ commuted our sentence. Do not forget what Paul writes to the Corinthians: "God was in Christ reconciling the world to Himself, not counting people's sins against them [but canceling them]" (2 Corinthians 5:19 AMP). Embrace it and live in the freedom that it was intended to give.

KEVIN HARTDIGE

You know, it is said that sin is the problem, but really it is the value and worth we assign to sin. We spend much of our Christian lives trying to avoid sinning. There is a tendency to magnify our problems, especially where sin is concerned, above and beyond the grace of God. "For the law was given through Moses, but grace and truth came through Jesus Christ" (John 1:17 NKJV). The problem is our inability to fully understand what it means that Jesus paid it all. I believe this is because once we have been saved by grace through faith, we have come to believe that the onus is now completely on us to maintain our salvation. Everything we do as believers is now under a magnifying glass, with everyone's eyes seemingly trained on our every move, hoping we do nothing that will bring disappointment to God and shame to the Church. This puts an incredible burden on us, one we were not meant to carry. The weight of this is not realized until we make a mistake, and we send ourselves to the altar to repent of our sin and promise to do better next time. We do everything we can to conform to the image of Jesus Christ and to renew our minds. Once we take on this responsibility that is reserved for the Holy Spirit, we thwart the good work that was begun in us and that is to be completed in our lives by Him, according to Philippians 1:6.

Thank God our salvation was not and is not contingent upon our goodness. Remember Romans 5:6–11. This fact is key to our identification. It is tremendously important that we see ourselves the way God sees us. Until we see what He sees, from His vantage point, we live out of our abilities trying to stay right before Him. If one acts like a Christian, doing what Christians do, then they are Christians, right? Behavior does not determine identity. It is understanding who we are in Christ that allows us to truly reflect His image here on earth. This allows us to rest in His finished work in appreciation of all that it means, without toiling for something He has already done. It is like the Pharisees who could not identify with Christ because they were too busy identifying with father Abraham and Moses the lawgiver, pursing their own righteousness. This is the mindset of those who take their salvation into their own hands. There are rules and regulations-twenty first century Ten Commandments-that keeps you focused on not falling instead of looking up to Jesus, the author and finisher of our faith. These rules were nailed to the cross at Calvary. Instead of realizing that Christs' sacrifice was enough we do everything to prevent from committing any infractions. Again, Pharisaical thinking refuses to be identified with Christ and keeps the responsibility of our salvation firmly in our own grasp and keeps us tied to things that remind us of our previous sins.

I personally could not reconcile who I was because of who others said I was and because of my lack of understanding who Christ proclaimed me to be. When you are taught that you are unworthy, you discount the value and worth that God the Father assigned to us when He created us in the beginning. We discount the value and worth He saw in us that made Him willing to redeem us. We discount the value and worth He has assigned to us presently that makes us His sons and daughters. Christians seem to like identifying themselves as sinners saved by grace. We are truly saved by grace, but once we have been saved, we no longer are identified as sinners but as saints. I think it becomes a type of false humility when we identify ourselves this way. If I committed an infraction against the rules then "my sin separates me from God" and I have to start over. The only thing that will keep us eternally separated from God is deciding to not place trust in Christ's once-for-all sacrifice. If I failed to tithe, I was robbing God and cursed with a curse. Kind of tough to be in Christ and cursed at the same time, don't you think? I believe there was a sincerity in being reminded through sermons to avoid sinning. It was necessary to help us in our sanctification process and keep us in right standing with Christ, so we thought. I sincerely wanted to be identified with Christ, and I believe others sincerely wanted me to be identified with Christ. This was simply the cost of staying saved and not forfeiting one's salvation. The reality is that when Christ receives us as His possession, we become a new creation and old things pass away (2 Corinthians 5:17). We are no longer identified by our past sins because Christ was made to be sin, so that we could be made the righteousness of God in Christ. We are now His ambassadors, His emissaries. This is our new identity.

CHAPTER 5 COGNITIVE DISSONANCE

Human beings typically maintain a consistency between their knowledge, their actions, and their attitudes. However, when there is a change in what one believes through the knowledge that one gains, there is typically a behavioral change that follows. This in turn creates a palpable tension that psychologists call cognitive dissonance. Cognitive dissonance creates discord between our actions and our attitudes. It creates a disruption in what we have previously believed and how we have previously behaved. To alleviate the existing tension, we make adjustments that will allow our beliefs, attitudes, and actions to realign (van Veen et al. 2009).

As we have discussed in an earlier chapter, much of what we embrace as our belief system is learned early on in childhood. This is critically important for us to understand because it is the foundation of our identity that becomes the impetus for how we live our lives. This was true for me and my beliefs and my understanding of God and the Bible, Christ and salvation, tithes and offering, sin and grace, and temptation and the devil. I think you get the idea. This is just a short list of the things that have affected or contributed to who I am today. Much of what I know and believed has remained intact, but there has been an evolution in what I had previously believed and understood about the grace of God specifically. For years and even today, it has been suggested by those charged with teaching us the Bible that the embracing of grace is ultimately a license to sin. The thought is that if there is no consequence for bad behavior, why would anyone try to live a saved life? People who think in this manner want us to be constantly thinking about how to avoid sin, instead of resting in what Christ accomplished with His death, burial, and resurrection. As a result we end up being sin conscious, which causes us to magnify sin over the power of the Holy Spirit who freed us from the power of sin when we accepted Him as Lord and Savior. We end up doing things (religious things) in relation to sin, as though we have to mitigate God's anger when we mess up. I really believe that many believe that these religious activities should merit favor from God and exempt them from any catastrophic events occurring in their lives. This attitude can be seen when bad things happen to "good" people.

That is the whole point of God's grace. In sending His Son to die on our behalf, He accomplished for us what we could not do for ourselves. We were deemed "not guilty" before a Holy God, who placed His wrath on Christ, the Lamb of God who takes away the sin of the world, according to John 1:29. God is not looking down low from on high, wishing and hoping we won't sin, as though He will be reticent to punish us when we do make a mistake. He wants us to live in the freedom of Christ's sacrifice. What I have come to learn and embrace concerning God's amazing grace has definitely created dissonance in my life. "The thief does not come except to steal, and to kill and to destroy. I have come that they may have life, and that they may have it more abundantly" (John 10:10 NKJV). The more I began to understand and embrace God's grace, the more I began to adjust my behavior to line up with what I have now learned, believed, and accepted about who I am. When who I am began to come into focus, I began to operate and live according to who I am in Christ, which in turn begins to lessen the tension. Grace erases fear. There is no more fear of sinning and disappointing God, or fellow humans for that matter. It has truly allowed me to love much and live abundantly.

CHAPTER 6 YIELDING TO TEMPTATION

Paul says, "And I testify again to every man who becomes circumcised that he is a debtor to keep the whole law. You have become estranged from Christ, you who attempt to be justified by the law; you have fallen from grace" (Galatians 5:3–4 NKJV). We used to sing a song when we were coming up that said, "Yield not to temptation because yielding is sin". What we were singing about was the belief that the devil could tempt us to make bad decisions and sin in the context of breaking one or more of the Ten Commandments and various other church prohibitions. This thinking caused us to spend our time constantly thinking about how to avoid doing anything that was considered sinful. Much of our time was spent looking for strategies to combat the onslaught of the enemy. Countless messages have been preached and countless books written that attempt to teach and train Christians how to not only recognize the attack of the enemy but also what to do to thwart his attacks. This is the real temptation, attempting to depend on one's own ability.

In Galatians, Paul talks to the saints about the fact that there is no profit to Gentiles becoming circumcised once they have come to faith in Christ. Listen to what he says earlier in Galatians in chapter 3: "O foolish Galatians! Who has bewitched you that you should not obey the truth, before whose eyes Jesus Christ was clearly portrayed among you as crucified? This only I want to learn from you; did you receive the Spirit by works of the law, or by the hearing of faith?" Are you so foolish? Having begun in the Spirit, are you now being made perfect by the flesh? The point is that Jesus Christ paid it all. His sacrifice alone has delivered us from the power and penalty of sin. Instead of looking for ways to supplement the work of Christ, we must trust and rely on that work and understand the magnitude, the totality, and the finality of Christ's death, burial, and resurrection and the resulting defeat of the entity who consumes much of our time and thoughts: the devil.

The Galatians were being taught, by Jews, that Christ's work was not enough to secure their salvation and that they needed to be circumcised. Paul lets them know that doing so—becoming circumcised—does not do anything but put them in bondage to the law, to obey it in its entirety. "Stand fast therefore in the liberty by which Christ has made us free, and do not be entangled again in a yoke of bondage."(Galatians 5:1, NKJV) This is what religion does; it enslaves us to rules and regulations that have no bearing on our salvation in terms of supplementing our salvation, or in terms of us gaining victory over sin. What it does do is cause us to fall from grace because we yield to the temptation to rely on our own efforts and not solely on Christ and His finished work. Religion speaks to self-effort, and urges people to make their own contribution to their righteousness and to maintain that righteousness. Religion keeps us on the treadmill of doing, ever trying to be good enough to earn God's favor and love. This is the deception of religion—the belief that man's efforts will, at some point, merit righteousness. What it does is cause us to compare ourselves with one another, using fellow Christians as the standard and measuring stick instead of God. This was Christ's main issue with the Pharisees and their desire to earn their own righteousness through observing the law, refusing to recognize Christ as the One who was to fulfill all righteousness and then give His righteousness to them. Whether we understand it or not, we have started out in faith, trusting God for salvation. Then, upon receiving His salvation, we seek our own righteousness through our religious efforts. But seek first the kingdom of God and His righteousness, and all these things will be added to you (Matthew 6:33 NKJV).

Jesus, while He was here on earth, was attempting to help the religious folk of His time stop focusing on the law and obtaining righteousness through its observance. Mike Kapler, in his book, *Clash of the Covenants*, does an excellent job of helping us understand that Jesus, in the Sermon on the Mount, was illustrating for His listeners the true letter of the law. He wanted them to understand the impossibility of being able to keep the law in its entirety. He wanted them to realize that God was providing a better way for them to be seen as righteous before the Father, a righteousness that would not come through observance of the law. I do not set aside the grace of God; for if righteousness comes through the law, then Christ died in vain (Galatians 2:21). Kapler says, "We find that when Jesus is asked a law-based question he will give a law based answer." When asked by the Rich Young Ruler what he needed to do to obtain eternal life, Jesus said, "Keep the commandments." The response from the young man was "I have been keeping them from my youth. What else do I need to do?" Sell everything, give the proceeds to the poor, and follow me, responded Jesus. Jesus was in essence saying if you want to pursue your own righteousness, this is what you must do, according to the law. Religion and the law of doing continue to demand more from us, claiming that what has already been given is not sufficient.

CHAPTER 7 GRACE

Webster's defines antithesis as "the direct opposite." Grace is the antithesis of the law. For the law was given through Moses, but grace and truth came through Jesus Christ (John 1:17 NKJV). The law was established under the Old Covenant. It was an exhaustive list of over six hundred commandments that God gave to Moses to give to the children of Israel. These conditions, if met by the people, would merit God's favor and keep them safe from their enemies. The salvation, and maintenance of said salvation, was dependent upon the ability of every man, woman, boy, and girl to adhere to the law, in its entirety, perfectly. The children of Israel, upon hearing this writ read aloud by Moses, replied, "All that the Lord has said we will do and be obedient" (Exodus 24:7 NKJV). Salvation in the hand of humans is an impossible mission. No matter how hard they tried, they were unable to succeed at perfect adherence to the law. In order to mitigate the consequences of their failures, they had to offer countless and varied sacrifices to God—sacrifices that would never be sufficient to appease the wrath of God. Therefore, by the deeds of the law, no flesh will be justified in His sight, for by the law is the knowledge of sin (Romans 3:20 NKJV).

Grace allows us to rest in the finished work of Christ for our redemption, for our justification, for our sanctification, for our salvation, and for our righteousness before God and our reconciliation to God. This is what the apostle Paul writes in Romans: "For when we were still without strength, in due time Christ died for the ungodly…But God demonstrates His own love toward us, in that while we were still sinners, Christ died for us…For if when we were enemies we were reconciled to God through the death of His Son, much more having been reconciled, we shall be saved by His life" (Romans 5:6, 8, 10 NKJV). Grace is truly amazing when you consider that it (grace) alone is sufficient for our salvation. Once we accept and embrace the sacrifice of Christ as our payment for sin, we are declared "not guilty." This frees us from the burden of trying to earn an early release from our bondage, by being good and demonstrating good behavior over a period of time. We never have to worry about being retried and sent back to serve out our previous sentence. The blood of Jesus Christ frees us from future condemnation. "That is, that God was in Christ reconciling the world to Himself, not imputing their trespasses to them (2 Corinthians 5:19 NKJV). Good news indeed.

Grace is love in action, the love of the Father that allowed His only begotten Son to die on our behalf. "There is no fear in love, but perfect love casts out fear, because fear involves torment. But he who fears has not been made perfect in love. We love Him because He first loved us" (1 John 4:18–19 NKJV). This is grace. When we operate our lives out of what others have determined as our identity, there will always be the presence of fear. In the movie *The Lion King*, fear caused Simba to run from his true identity and purpose. Simba's uncle Scar had convinced him that he was responsible for an unthinkable evil, labeling him a murderer. What Simba failed to realize was that as a son, he was the rightful heir to all that his father possessed, including the right to reign. Consumed by fear, and of being found out, he began to function outside of his true identity. And even though he thought he was living a life of leisure and freedom, Simba had to submit to the dos and don'ts of his new living arrangement. Fear robs us of our true identity, an identity given to us from before the foundation of the world. This is because when we begin to live our lives outside of what God intended for us, we actually spend much of our lives performing, hoping that what we do is acceptable to others. When we embrace who we are in Christ, we are immediately accepted by Him, and there is no need for us to perform in order to be pleasing to Him. Fear's goal is deception. His perfect love for us eradicates the fear that constantly tells us that we need to do more and that we need to be more. When fear is an influencer in our lives, it becomes difficult to accept and live in God's abundant grace because it does not trust completely what has been perfectly accomplished through Christ.

The goal of God's love for us is unfettered and uninterrupted relationship and fellowship with Him. Hear the words of the Apostle John: "Behold what manner of love the Father has bestowed on us, that we should be called children of God! Therefore the world does not know us, because it did not know Him. Beloved, now we are children of God; and it has not yet been revealed what we shall be, but we know that when He is revealed, we shall be like Him, for we shall see Him as He is" (1 John 3:1–2 NKJV). Even while Christ walked the earth as a human, He pursued relationships with those to whom He ministered—the twelve disciples, Lazarus, Martha, and Mary. John, in the Gospel bearing his name, describes himself in the third person as the disciple whom Jesus loves. God chose relationship with Abram and made his descendants, the Israelites, His special people. God, at the beginning of time as we know it, was in relationship with Adam before he was deceived by the devil to go against God's command. The Church is the bride of Christ. The reality is that God the Father loved the entire world so much that He gave His son to ensure that we could always be in relationship with him. It is our trust in the perfect and sinless life of Christ that enables His amazing grace to infuse us with His life. I have come that they may have life, and that they may have it more abundantly. So, get busy living…

EPILOGUE

Grace is what happens when a Holy God decides to, for no other reason but love, wrap Himself in flesh, come to the world that He created, and give His life in order to redeem and reconcile His creation unto Himself so that we can reside in His infinite love forever. This love cannot be earned; it cannot be lost. There is nothing in this world that can be compared to the love demonstrated by God toward us. His love is perfectly selfless, and this love has been poured into our hearts by the Holy Spirit. This allows us to connect to Him spiritually and return love to Him and extend love to others. If you are anything like me, living as a Christian was a bit of a challenge. I did not know how to accept the love He intended for me because I didn't see Him as a loving father. Everything about being a Christian said that I had to perform for His acceptance, His approval, and His love.

This was because I did not see myself the same way that He sees me, as a son. He chose us in Him before the foundation of the world, that we should be holy and without blame before Him in love, having predestined us to adoption as sons by Jesus Christ to Himself, according to the good pleasure of His will, to the praise of the glory of His grace, by which He made us accepted in the Beloved (Ephesians 1:4–6 NKJV). Instead, I saw myself and identified with the person I thought I was supposed to be according to others. At the end of the day, my presentation was not in sync with who I was meant to be.

Sometime in 2005 I heard one of the ministers ask God to enlighten the eyes of the understanding of the individual for whom she was praying, according to Ephesians 1:18. For me, this was a life changer. I began to read and then pray this for myself. Since that time the Father has been peeling away the calloused layers of my heart and revealing to me my true identity in Him. "Behold what manner of love the Father has bestowed on us, that we should be called children of God! Therefore the world does not know us, because it did not know Him. Beloved, now we are children of God; and it has not yet been revealed what we shall be, but we know that when He is revealed, we shall be like Him, for we shall see Him as He is. And everyone who has this hope in Him purifies himself, just as He is pure" (1 John 3:1–3 NKJV). His love for us is immense, doing for us what we could not do for ourselves. I am learning to rest in that love and allow His love to be manifested through me to others. Years ago, a pastor came to the church I was then attending, Tower of Faith Evangelistic Church in Compton, California. I believe this was during a Founders Week meeting for our church. His name was Tony Williams, and I will never forget something he said concerning grace. He said, "Grace is the empowering presence of God in our lives enabling us to be all He has created us to be and to do all He has created us to do." He empowers us to live according to His purpose, by the Holy Spirit. You don't have to make it up, just rest in who He is and you will be His true representation on the earth.

Embrace Grace

Many have understood the definition of Grace simply as unmerited favor from God. I agree with this definition wholeheartedly, as there is nothing any of us - past, present or future - has done or could ever do to deserve or earn his favor This limited definition, however, does little to paint a vivid portrait of how dynamic, how amazingly beautiful, and how encompassing His Grace truly is. The Apostle John, in the Gospel bearing his name wrote, "For out of His fullness [the superabundance of His grace and truth] we have all received grace upon grace [spiritual blessing upon spiritual blessing, favor upon favor, and gift heaped upon gift]. For the Law was given through Moses, but grace [the unearned, undeserved favor of God] and truth came through Jesus Christ. (John 1: 16AMP).

Grace, my friends, has a name and a face, a real identity; Jesus Christ the Messiah. I hope that you will truly come to understand Grace and His significance. As you come to understand this, I pray that you will learn to embrace his Grace and live a life of love and abundance. Why embrace, you ask? Because I believe that an embrace is more than just a hug. It is taking or receiving gladly or eagerly; it is accepting willingly; and availing oneself (dictionary.com). The embracing of Grace is the embracing of Jesus Christ, which frees us to enjoy our lives in a way we may never have thought possible; freeing us from the fear and the condemnation associated with religion that is always pointing us back to our shortcomings and our need to do more. "In this is love, not that we loved God, but that He loved us and sent His Son to be the propitiation [that is, the atoning sacrifice, and the satisfying offering] for our sins [fulfilling God's requirement for justice against sin and placating His wrath]. 1 John 4:10, AMP

When we embrace Grace we'll learn to rest and reside in the peace of God. When we embrace Grace, the abundance and love that is His, becomes ours, and we experience life as He intended because we are now in communion and fellowship with Him. As a result, we reverence Him but we don't fear Him, because His perfect love removes all fear. He makes his abode with us so we are ever in His presence. When we embrace Grace we take up residence in His love. Everything we will ever need exists in Him. Paul, writing to the Romans says, "And we know [with great confidence] that God [who is deeply concerned about us] causes all things to work together [as a plan] for good for those who love God, to those who are called according to His plan and purpose. (Romans 8:28 AMP). When you embrace His Grace you will find yourself residing in His Love and Abundance.

Identity: the condition of being oneself or itself, and not another.

The condition or character as to who a person is or what a thing is; the qualities, beliefs, etc., that distinguish or identify a person or thing.

(Identity, Dictionary.com, 2019)

REFERENCES

van Veen, V., M. K. Krug, J. W. Schooler, and C. S. Carter. 2009. Neural activity predicts attitude change in cognitive dissonance. Nature Neuroscience 12(11): 1469–1474. https://doi-org.lopesalum.idm.oclc.org/10.1038/ nn.2413

Kapler, Michael C. 2018. Clash of the Covenants: Escaping Religious Bondage Through the Grace Guarantee.

9 7989 8973 1909